ANDREW LLOYD WEBBER'S

ALTO SAXOPHONE

The PHANTOM of the OPERA

CONTENTS

Music by ANDREW LLOYD WEBBER
Lyrics by CHARLES HART
Additional lyrics by RICHARD STILGOE
Title song: lyrics by CHARLES HART,
Additional lyrics by RICHARD STILGOE & MIKE BATT
Book by RICHARD STILGOE & ANDREW LLOYD WEBBER

The Phantom played by MICHAEL CRAWFORD
Christine played by SARAH BRIGHTMAN   Raoul played by STEVE BARTON

THINK OF ME

(From "THE PHANTOM OF THE OPERA")

Music by ANDREW LLOYD WEBBER
Lyrics by CHARLES HART
Additional lyrics by RICHARD STILGOE

Alto Saxophone

ANGEL OF MUSIC
(From "THE PHANTOM OF THE OPERA")

Music by ANDREW LLOYD WEBBER
Lyrics by CHARLES HART
Additional lyrics by RICHARD STILGOE

Alto Saxophone

THE PHANTOM OF THE OPERA

Music by ANDREW LLOYD WEBBER
Lyrics by CHARLES HART
Additional Lyrics by RICHARD STILGOE and MIKE BATT

Alto Saxophone

THE MUSIC OF THE NIGHT
(From "THE PHANTOM OF THE OPERA")

Music by ANDREW LLOYD WEBBER
Lyrics by CHARLES HART
Additional lyrics by RICHARD STILGOE

Alto Saxophone

7

PRIMA DONNA
(From "THE PHANTOM OF THE OPERA")

Music by ANDREW LLOYD WEBBER
Lyrics by CHARLES HART
Additional lyrics by RICHARD STILGOE

Alto Saxophone

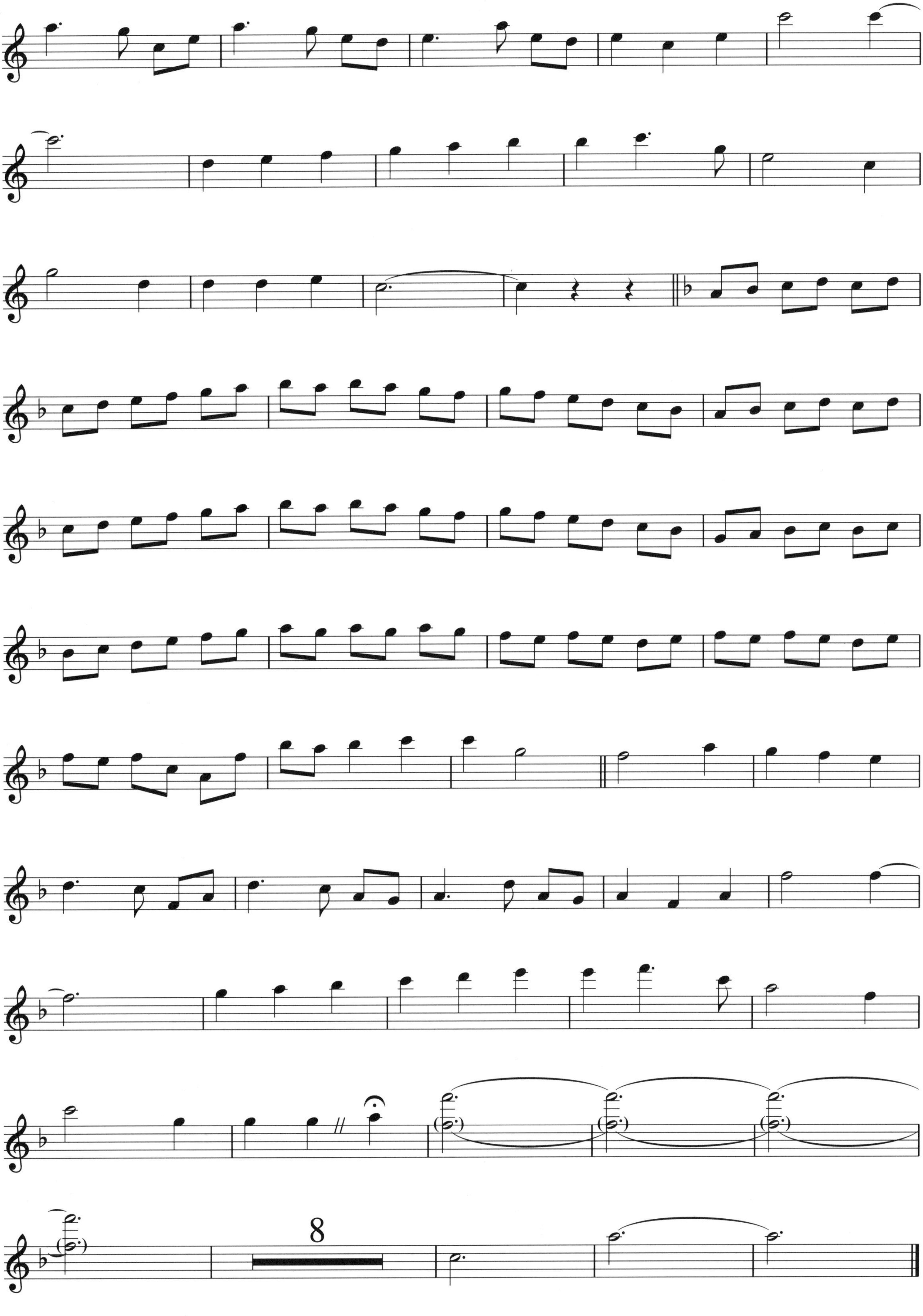
8

ALL I ASK OF YOU
(From "THE PHANTOM OF THE OPERA")

Music by ANDREW LLOYD WEBBER
Lyrics by CHARLES HART
Additional lyrics by RICHARD STILGOE

Alto Saxophone

Moderately Slow

11

MASQUERADE
(From "THE PHANTOM OF THE OPERA")

Music by ANDREW LLOYD WEBBER
Lyrics by CHARLES HART
Additional lyrics by RICHARD STILGOE

Alto Saxophone

13

THE POINT OF NO RETURN
(From "THE PHANTOM OF THE OPERA")

Music by ANDREW LLOYD WEBBER
Lyrics by CHARLES HART
Additional lyrics by RICHARD STILGOE

Alto Saxophone

WISHING YOU WERE SOMEHOW HERE AGAIN
(From "THE PHANTOM OF THE OPERA")

Music by ANDREW LLOYD WEBBER
Lyrics by CHARLES HART
Additional lyrics by RICHARD STILGOE

Alto Saxophone